"WHAT AM I DOING IN A STEP-FAMILY?"

Written by Claire Berman
Illustrated by Dick Wilson. Designed by Paul Walter

First Carol Publishing Group Edition 1992

A Lyle Stuart Book
Published by Carol Publishing Group
Lyle Stuart is a registered trademark of Carol Communications, Inc.

Editorial Offices : 600 Madison Avenue, New York, NY 10022
Sales & Distribution Offices: 120 Enterprise Avenue, Secaucus, NJ 07094
In Canada: Canadian Manda Group, P.O. Box 920, Station U, Toronto,
Ontario, M8Z 5P9, Canada

Queries regarding rights and permissions should be addressed to Carol
Publishing Group, 600 Madison Avenue, New York, NY 10022

Manufactured in the United States of America
ISBN 0-8184-0563-5

Typesetting by Ella-Type, Hollywood, California
Mechanicals by Harry Robinson

Carol Publishing Group books are available at special discounts
for bulk purchases, for sales promotions, fund raising, or
educational purposes. Special editions can also be created to
specifications. For details contact: Special Sales Department,
Carol Publishing Group, 120 Enterprise Ave., Secaucus, NJ 07094

10 9 8 7 6 5 4   3   2   1

Library of Congress Cataloging-in-Publication Data

Berman, Claire.
    What am I doing in a stepfamily?

     Summary: Advice for children of divorced or remarried parents on
adjusting to life with a stepfamily.
        1. Stepchildren--Juvenile literature. 2. Stepparents--Juvenile
literature. 3. Children of divorced parents--Juvenile literature.
[1. Stepparents. 2. Divorce. 3. Remarriage] 1. Wilson, Dick,
1930-   ill.   II. Title.
HQ777.7.B48   1982   306.8'74   82-16760

For Orin, Mitch and Eric
With special thanks to Carole Livingston and Dr. James Meltzer

Let's begin at the beginning.

There once was a time when you lived in a once-upon-a-time family with your mother and your father. It was a lot like the families in story books – the ones with a mama bear, a papa bear and a baby bear living in the same house. Only, of course, your home was filled with people, not bears. And this family was very special – because it was yours.

Like most of us, you probably never stopped to think about your family – except to wonder what they were going to give you on your birthday…or if your parents would let you stay up ("Just this one time, please") to watch a cartoon special on television. You weren't surprised when your parents said "Okay." That's because most of us know what we can and what we can't get away with in our own families.

We understand how our families work.

But what happens if your family changes? Suppose one day you find you're in a new kind of family – one that even has a special name. It is called a "stepfamily." Suddenly, there's a lot about your family you don't understand.

Some of the people in this new family are the same ones as in the old one. First of all, there's you. (And your brothers and your sisters, if you've got any.)

You live – probably most of the time – with the same mom or dad. But you no longer live with both of your parents at the same time.

What has happened? Your mom or your dad – or maybe both of them – has a new husband or wife now, someone who is very important in your new and different family.

It seems pretty confusing – and it is. So many questions are going through your mind. You stop and ask yourself:

"What am I doing in a stepfamily, anyway?"

Boys and girls become members of stepfamilies in a number of ways. Let's look at some of them.

Most children find themselves in stepfamilies after the mother and father in their first family are divorced.

"Divorce" is not a happy word. When your parents used that word, they were saying that your family would be different from the way it used to be. No, you wouldn't have to give up your pet hamster. That's not the kind of different we're talking about. But there would be lots of changes. The big change is that your parents no longer would live together as husband and wife.

Where would that leave you? Most of the time, you would make your home with either your mother or your father – but not with both of them together.

That's not the way once-upon-a-time stories are supposed to happen. (Who ever heard of Mama Bear getting a divorce from Papa Bear?) However divorce is something that happens to millions of real-life families. In Los Angeles, California, for example, there are more than 1,000 divorces each and every week. And with 52 weeks to a year, that adds up to 52,000 divorces a year in only one city... in one state...in one country...in the whole world. That's a lot of divorces to think about!

And that's why many girls and boys (just like you) and women and men (like your parents) spend a lot of time trying to understand divorce – and how and why it happened to them.

When your mom and dad married, they loved each other – and they thought they always would. They felt so good about being together that they started a family. That's why they had you. (And your sisters and brothers.)

They hoped all of you would live happily ever after – together.

But that isn't the way things worked out. People change. Even you. You're not the same person you were when you were younger, are you? When you were little, you couldn't reach the shelf in the kitchen – the one that held the cookie jar. Now you're bigger and there's no need to ask for help when you feel like having a cookie.

When you were younger, your very best friend was Jonathan who lived down the street. But your feelings change about people. Now you think Jonathan is a jerk!

Your mother and father changed, too. As they grew older, they may have discovered that they no longer enjoyed the same things. Being together didn't make them happy. They may have tried to stay together for a while. After all, they knew that being married and having children was a serious matter.

Because your parents weren't happy with each other, nobody in the family could feel

very good. Finally, your parents decided it would be better for them to get a divorce.... And that's what they did.

Remember: <u>They didn't divorce you</u>! Your mother is no longer your father's wife, but she is still your mom. Your father is no longer your mother's husband, but he is still your dad. They are both your parents – and they always will be. You will always be their child. The divorce didn't change <u>that</u>.

Sometimes, families change because one of the parents has died. That is very sad. You miss having a mother or father to help you grow up. You miss the happy times – like when you all went to the circus. But you seem also to forget the not-so-happy times that are part of every family, too. You wish your life was the way it used to be.

That wish can't come true. Instead, what <u>can</u> happen (and often does) is that your parent who is still alive meets new people and makes new friends – just as you do. In time, your parent may like one of these new friends enough to decide to marry again. This special friend then becomes your stepparent, and your family is larger once again.

Having a stepparent doesn't mean anyone expects you to forget your mom or dad who has died. But if all you remember are the fun times, it is hard to accept your stepparent – who takes you to the park but also reminds you to do your homework and practice the piano...and is somebody less perfect than an angel.

People aren't angels. Angels are angels. If people were angels, T-shirts would come with cutouts for wings. People aren't devils, either.

Of course you knew this. Still, when you learned your parent was getting married again, you probably wondered:

What will my stepparent be like?

Many children have the idea that a stepparent is someone who is strict. That's because they have heard all about Cinderella's stepmother. She was terrible! Do you know that story? Then you remember that Cinderella also had a fairy godmother who made all her wishes come true. She sent Cinderella to the ball where she met her prince, and the story has a very happy ending.

Sometimes we forget that Cinderella is only a story. Cinderella's stepmother is make-believe. So is her fairy godmother. In real life, most stepparents are <u>not</u> wicked people. Nor are they fairy godmothers. They are real people who are often good, sometimes not so good...just like your own mother or father... just like you.

And they have feelings. Just as you do. Do you know something? They've probably been worrying and wondering about what kind of child <u>you</u> are – and how you will treat them!

So there are questions going around in everyone's mind. Would you be interested in what other kids in stepfamilies think about?

Here's what kids want to know:

What should I call my stepparent?

This simple question can get all mixed up. You know what you <u>won't</u> do. You aren't going to bow or curtsy. And you can't keep calling your stepparent "Er" either.

But what do you do if your stepparent expects you to call her "Mom" when you already have a mother? And what should you say if your mother asks you to call her new husband "Daddy" – and you think that would make your own father unhappy?

A good idea is to talk it over with your parents and stepparents. It's important to find out how they feel. And ask yourself what makes <u>you</u> comfortable, too. If you don't feel right calling two people "Daddy," don't do it. Some children find it easy to call their father "Dad" and their stepfather "Pop." Or the other way around. Others call their stepparent by his or her first name.

Remember, it isn't what you call someone that's important. It's how you feel about the person that matters.

May I call you Bill?

What if my stepparent has children too?

Chances are, these children are busy wondering about you. Like you, they know there will be some changes. The new house may be crowded, and you may end up sharing a room with your stepbrother or stepsister...and maybe their Great Dane, too. There's something else you will have to share – your parent's attention.

Don't be surprised if there are arguments. (We'd be amazed if there were not.) Now, be honest. Don't you ever argue with your own sister or brother? Of course you do. And you've known them your whole life! Here's something else to keep in mind: don't be embarrassed to make up.

It takes a while for people (big or little) to learn to live together. It doesn't happen overnight. Everyone has to work at it, and sometimes it can take months or even years.

Be patient. It's worth it. In time you may find you have gained more than new step-brothers and stepsisters. With a little luck and a lot of understanding all around, they also may become your very good friends.

There's something else you ought to know about stepfamilies, and this is a good time to make it clear: Children and their stepparents and their stepbrothers and stepsisters don't have to love each other right away – or even ever. They ought to try to get along. Often, getting along grows into loving. It's nice when that happens.

What if the grownups play favorites?

You may think the big people in the family aren't being fair. Why is it that your stepparent makes a fuss when you do something (like not putting the milk container back in the refrigerator when you're through with it), but the same person can actually trip over his own child's roller skates and act as if he doesn't even see them? You think your stepparent favors his child.

You're probably right. After all, he has known his child longer – in the same way your parent knows you best and loves you. We bet you act differently with your stepparent than you do with your own mom and dad.

People who have lived in stepfamilies for a while say that when everyone gets to know each other, the game of playing favorites comes to an end.

Do I have to do what my stepparent tells me?

You don't always agree with your own mom or dad, and we guess there are also times when you won't want to listen to your stepparent. Suppose your stepmother asks you to take the dog for a walk and you don't feel like going out.

"I don't have to listen," you may think. "She's not my mother."

Here is what your stepmother may be thinking: "It's his dog. I'm not going to take care of it. I'm not the maid."

Who exactly <u>are</u> the two of you?

You're people who live in the same home (at least some of the time) and who both have very good taste because you love the same person – who happens to be your mom or dad. You can make your parent much happier if you and your stepparent do listen to each other – and help each other. (Chances are, you'll feel better too.)

Will I know how to behave in my stepfamily?

Figuring out the rules of your new home will not be easy. Think of it this way. Everybody lives according to rules. "Cross when the light is green" is one. "Don't walk on the grass" is another.

Families live according to rules, too. Except that these rules aren't the kind you see written on signs. In your home, for example, the children may have to set the table for dinner. Another rule could be that you have to finish all of your homework before watching TV. You may not like all your family's rules, but at least you know what is expected of you.

The hard part about joining a new family is not knowing, at first, what the rules are. Some may be the same as the ones you were used to…and many will be different. Some will make you angry (you've always been able to stay in bed and read – and now you find that "lights out" means "turn your lights out – <u>right now!</u>"), and some will make you glad ("You mean it's okay to have a guinea pig – oh, wow!"). But until you learn the rules and accept them, life could be very complicated.

We've talked a lot about rules because we know it isn't easy for two families to get together and become one. It takes hard work. There's a big word for learning to get along. That word is "compromise."

Compromise means each person in a new family will have to stop being stubborn about old and new rules and learn to give in at least a little bit. In time, everyone will be clear about the rules of the new family. Then all of you can stop thinking about them so much.

I don't live with my stepfamily. What will happen when I visit?

A good present to receive, after your parents are divorced, may be your very own suitcase. (You're thinking, "You call that a present?") You need a suitcase because you may be going back and forth from one parent to the other.

Traveling can be fun. Here's what else it can be: confusing.

At first, the idea of visiting your own parent may seem strange. You thought you understood about visits. They meant getting all dressed up to spend time with your Aunt Zelda – and remembering not to jump up and down on her sofa. But this kind of visit is different. It means getting ready to see someone you used to live with every day of the week – even when both of you were in pajamas.

You feel mixed up. Sometimes it takes a while after you wake up for you to remember whose house you're in. Is it your mom's or your dad's? And which one has the closet that holds your blue sweater?

Why is it that, whenever it rains, your green boots with the yellow laces are at the "other house"? (Here's an idea: Ask your parents to buy two pairs of boots. That way you can leave one pair in each home.) When your parent remarries, you also must get used to there being different people in each home.

Some mornings you may lie in bed wondering: Where <u>do</u> I belong?

The answer is simple. You belong with both families – because both of them love you – even if most of the time you live with one parent and only visit your other parent.

Visiting can take place as often as several times a week...or as once-in-a-while as during holidays and school vacations.

It's hard to figure out what to do or what is expected of you in a special-times home. Do you bring along your work or leave your schoolbooks at home? May you pour a glass of apple juice or must you ask permission? Is it alright to invite a friend to sleep over?

Don't try to guess the answers. If you have questions about what the people in this home expect, <u>ask them.</u> It's also a good idea to tell your stepparent how <u>you</u> feel about things.

If you like a light on outside your room at night, say so. Do you turn blue if the teensiest piece of onion peeks out from your spaghetti sauce? Let your stepparent know that. Guessing games can be fun, but people trying to be a family have a better time when they don't have to guess about each other.

Will I have my own space?

You may find your stepfamily's home pretty crowded and it may not be possible for you to have a room of your own – especially if you'll be using it only some of the time. But it's not fun to have to take everything back and forth with you whenever you come and go. (Remember, we said you need a suitcase – not a trunk!)

It's a good idea to talk to your parent and stepparent about setting aside a special space for you in their home. A shelf or a closet might do it. Or even a few drawers or a small chest – just as long as it's yours.

Your stepfamily will feel good when they look at your space and think that you'll be coming to visit again. And you will like knowing that some of your things – your books, special toys and even those green boots – are waiting for your return.

Will my parent be sad if I like my stepparent?

Now that you have your own space and know the rules of your new family, you can relax – and even enjoy it!

It's fun to discover that your stepmom is a champion at checkers. Once in a while when you play her, you actually win! But then you begin to worry: If I like my stepmother, won't my own mother feel sad? You think about this so much that when you go home, you don't even want to talk about the visit.

There are times when you may need to be by yourself. Most often it's a good idea to share your feelings with those who care about you. Of course you can talk to your mom or dad about your visit. Your parents want you to be happy. If you tell them you like – or love – your stepparent, it won't change the way your own parents feel about you. (After all, your love hasn't changed for your parent, has it?)

What you are learning is that we can love different people in different ways.

Here's something else that's very important. Even though it's a good idea to talk about your visits, you don't have to tell about <u>everything</u>. Your mom or dad, or even your stepparent, may ask a lot of questions about what goes on in that "other house." If you think you should not be telling, don't answer. Each of your families is entitled to its privacy, and you are not a reporter. You're not a detective, either. If the grownups are curious, let them find out the answers to their questions some other way.

If my parent and stepparent have a baby, what will that make me?

You then become an older brother or sister. People may explain that the baby is your half-brother or half-sister. That simply means you and the baby have one parent who's the same and one who is different. It doesn't mean there has to be any "half" in how you feel about the baby. A brother or sister can be a <u>whole</u> lot of joy.

At first, you may not know whether or not to be happy about the baby. You're probably wondering if the baby will change the way your parent feels about you.

Remember, we said you were born when your parents were happy to become a family. Now your mom or dad (and their new husband or wife) have made the same decision. This time they <u>know</u> about the pleasure there is in having a child – because they know you.

The baby will not change the way your parent feels about you. If you have sisters and brothers, you already know that mothers and fathers are able to love more than one child. Now you are finding out that children can love more than one set of parents.

Belonging to a stepfamily means there are more people in your life. More sisters and brothers, including the step ones. More people you think of as grandparents and aunts and uncles. More cousins. More neighbors and friends. That means many new names to learn. And a sack full of cards to receive on your birthday.

Getting to know and like so many people (and having them like you) is one of the best parts of what being in a stepfamily – <u>your</u> stepfamily – is all about.

Books in this delightful series...

"WHERE DID I COME FROM?" by Peter Mayle and Arthur Robins. The facts of life without any nonsense and with illustrations.

"WHAT'S HAPPENING TO ME?" by Peter Mayle and Arthur Robins. A guide to puberty, from the authors of "WHERE DID I COME FROM?"

"WHY DO I HAVE TO WEAR GLASSES?" by Sandra Lee Stuart and Arthur Robins.

"WHY AM I GOING TO THE HOSPITAL?" by Claire Ciliotta, Carole Livingston and Dick Wilson. A helpful guide to a new experience.

"WHY WAS I ADOPTED?" by Carole Livingston and Arthur Robins. The facts of adoption with love and illustrations.

"WHAT AM I DOING IN A STEPFAMILY?" by Claire Berman and Dick Wilson. How two families can be better than one.

HOW TO BE A PREGNANT FATHER by Peter Mayle and Arthur Robins. An illustrated survival guide for the father-to-be.

Each book is delightfully written and illustrated in the style of the book you hold in your hands!

Ask for these books at your bookseller. If your bookseller can't supply you, order directly from the publisher by calling 1-800-447-BOOK. And send for our complete catalog of titles: Carol Publishing Group, 120 Enterprise Ave., Secaucus, NJ 07094.

You'll be glad you did!